CHILDHOOD IN WARTIME KEELE

Poems of Reminiscence

by

PHILIP HIGSON

The Friarswood Press

© Copyright, 1995, by Philip John Willoughby-Higson
ISBN: 0 9525835 0 X

Published by The Friarswood Press,
1 Westlands Avenue, Newcastle, Staffordshire. ST5 2PU
and printed by Prontaprint,
Queen's Parade, Ryecroft, Newcastle, Staffordshire. ST5 1RW

CONTENTS

Dedication — iv

Author's Preface — v

The Poems:

Biggles on Fridays	1
Warriors in Arcady	2
Midsummer Cornfield	4
The Collective Launching	6
The Vicar Taking Scripture	8
Intimations of Immorality	10
The Truant	12
Vanished Ghosts	13
Remains of the old 'Three Mile'	14
Country Retrospect	15
Keele Revisited	16
Shadows	16
Aubade	17
December Landscape	18

Illustrations:

The author as a Keele Schoolboy	Cover
The Riley often seen in Keele	7
The old Keele Village School	9
Students exploring Keele Village	18
The author as a Liverpool Ph.D.	Cover

TO

THE GODDESS OF MY SONNETS,

who passed into a different dimension

on the 24th of March 1993,

but who remains my spiritual ally still.

Author's Preface

From 1941 to 1943 I was a pupil at the old Keele Village School built in Victorian times by Ralph Sneyd, uncle and namesake of the last squire of Keele. Although my people resided in Newcastle, I had a great-aunt at Madeley Heath and, as a result of a family arrangement to ensure the greater safety of its younger members, I spent periods of the War at her bungalow there. Thus, beside making friends with fellow-pupils at Keele School, I belonged to the 'gang' of Madeley Heath youngsters (then including an evacuee of two) who swarmed over Vincent Hunt's farm, 'helped' with the harvesting of his corn, 'flew' over Nazi Germany in a gnarled oak near his byre, and drilled and marched near our 'den' on Agger Hill. In Newcastle I can remember the War coming uncomfortably close when an Air Raid Warden told my family that a German bomb, which had apparently jammed in its rack, would probably have scored a direct hit on our house. But we had another close brush with the conflict at Madeley Heath when in broad daylight a Hurricane fighter with guns blazing swept low overhead in pursuit of a Heinkel which it succeeded in shooting down.

In Keele the most dramatic evidence that we were at war was the sudden arrival of a host of gum-chewing and cigar-smoking American soldiers who commandeered the park and seemed to spend most of their time buzzing about in absurdly diminutive jeeps. There was a degree of hero-worship for these genial newcomers on the part of the village schoolkids, but some of us seem to have resented their presence a little for I can remember being second-in-command of an élite unit of ten-year-olds obsessed with stalking the sentries through the dense undergrowth which then reached to the park gates. At least there was no confusion of allegiances when one of our teachers, Miss Jenkins, read to us from the innumerable 'Biggles' books which then flooded the market. This happened every Friday afternoon, and she was able to blackmail us into good behaviour during the rest of the week with the threat that it would not! The two school headmistresses from my time – Miss Tennant and Miss Downend – spring briefly to life in the pages that follow, and an extremely vague and ethereal vicar wanders in to give another of his less than electrifying lessons in Divinity.

I remember with profound gratitude the stern but benign and immensely conscientious régime at the village school; and, as for the limitless playground of fields and lanes into which we pupils were released at lunchtime, I there found an ecstatic sense of harmony with my environment which I have rarely been privileged to experience since. To the right of the track leading out of the village towards Quarry Bank was a large cornfield where I would adore listening to skylarks in the baking midsummer heat before going to slake my thirst at the clumsy iron pump behind the 'Sneyd Arms'. The memory of that experience remained with me until, some forty years later, I recorded it in 'Midsummer Cornfield' – undoubtedly one of the happiest poems I have produced in a lifetime. Many other memories lingered, too, waiting to surface and console me and be gratefully written down at less congenial times – times of heartbreak and overwork when, as a lecturer in the humanities who embraced Ciceronian ideals, I was treated with ever more overt contempt. It was always on the same brief period of country childhood that I drew for solace, nothing else in the first quarter-century of my life having affected or enriched me so much.

We pupils were an astonishingly mixed lot – from well-scrubbed and smartly dressed townees to village lads with cropped heads and huge spark-striking clogs – yet we made up a sort of human totality simply because we were so varied; and we gelled together partly perhaps because, like the rest of the country, we had for a while an obvious common enemy. At the time, unspeakable horrors were being perpetrated and sufferings endured, but in Keele as in many another nook of England the team was pulling as one, the pompous and the worthless were discarded and merit was given a chance, and everything had a more genuine feel to it. The human animal while fighting Hitler, if only by keeping in being a society with nobler ideals than his, possessed a dignity which was undeniable and could be read in almost every face. We had of course our knaves and our buffoons, and my memories of wartime Keele are not entirely free of either, but even where these appear and give my writing something of a satirical edge, that edge is softened by the deep happiness of the schoolchild observing them, and perhaps by the feeling that even they were part of a species engaged in an admirable and historic task.

P.J.W-H.

*Newcastle-under-Lyme,
March, 1995.*

Biggles on Fridays

He was part of the weaponry of our war,
                the fibre of our pride,
The equal of Churchill, and of Shakespeare,
A stiffener of sinew and summoner of blood
Heartening the old in an ageing, trembling nation,
                no less than the young they read him to,
                the precarious inheritors.
His deeds left vapour-trails of wonderment,
flashes off Spitfires' wings that our eyes still witness,
divings out of the sun to surprise our foe,
a hawk's stare through the sights, a tensing wait
with finger poised on the button of pulsing death.

In our rustic nest of scholarship bathed in green,
he was the star-turn, he united us
as none of those inky everyday rituals could
that only served to separate blithe from blundering;
he recruited us all, the teachers with the taught,
                into his murderous squadron
flying in formation, alert and resourceful,
                knowing that we should win.
No-one was dull then, no-one then was backward,
Everyone sparkled with his rare charisma
                and dared not fail the leader.

If some habitual maverick at those times
                got one wing out of place,
twitched in a manner suggesting inattention
and insufficient awe of the laurelled hero,
our thrilled narrator, now a being transformed –
as vibrant as a 'cello and English as Elgar –
would turn on him, like an airborne cannonade,
deadly staccato bursts of withering ire.

Bigglesworth, Algy, Ginger, and monocled Bertie
might threaten then for a hideous sickening moment
to stall into silence with the book slammed to

      and the miscreant saboteur condemned to groan
                beneath corporate vengeance later.
    It rarely came to this. But the threat – what a weapon!
    The most feared, the most telling in teacher's armoury;
    That artful dame who used our beloved leader
              as her private ally too!

Warriors in Arcady

Strange how that giant war coloured our distant Eden:
We were children exploring field and pond, quarry and woodland,
Making our secret den in a dense bush on the tilt of Agger Hill,
Yet we became a platoon with tin-hats and weaponry,
Precisely graded ranks, and solemn drill;
We practised fieldcraft, without calling it by name,
And stalked the Yankee sentries at Keele Hall gates
Burrowing through neglected engulfing undergrowth
Quite convinced that if they detected our trespass
In that high-walled world of dappled shadow that was
The old Squire's park, they would take aim and fire.
They never noticed us, but slouched in pleated tunics –
Nearer to lounge-suits than the English Tommy's garb –
And were genial to other 'kids' who, ignoring our private war,
Went up to the enemy, made friends, and were plied
With gum, and U.S. buttons, and perhaps took
A long dizzying draw on a fat cigar, or Turkish cigarette.
Our platoon, though, never compromised with these intruders,
Though we marvelled at their neat and dinky jeeps
That buzzed about, carrying umpteen times their weight
In Americans; braking, jerking, veering, but incredibly
Never toppling their enormous lolling load.
We watched, but held aloof from, all this strangeness,
Perhaps somehow aware that it had no part
In our village's ancient feudal stability.

But we *were* involved. We were involved too in the
Battle for the skies: readers of 'spotter' books,

Connoisseurs of aircraft sagely instructing our seniors; and
Breathless adherents of Squadron Leader Bigglesworth,
That airborne Homeric hero, a fiction but real to us.

And then came the day when his world swooped suddenly close
In innocent sunlight, Hurricane chasing Heinkel
Over sleepy startled fields where cattle grazed,
Pursuer and pursued flying low, towards Madeley village,
The attacker's staccato fire riddling the foe,
Striking home, bringing him down with a ghastly crunch.
Then, the instant exhibit, guarded by Constable Buckley
Ad hoc Museum Curator, was examined by us all –
A glasshouse-nosed one hundred and eleven fighter
Crumpled beyond repair. Biggles had come and gone,
Leaving his litter, without a second glance.

Small wonder that the oak against Hunt's farm
Into which we had clambered many a time before,
A gnarled and knotted and idiosyncratic growth,
Became our bomber and carried us over the Ruhr,
Starstruck and lost in flight, giving reports
One to another, perched high in the branches:
A steady drone-drone coming from the pilot,
Nice calculations from the navigator,
The occasional burst of fire from the poor rear-gunner
In danger of being emulsified by attackers.

We lived it all. We were patriots and a half,
And I for one was a ten-year-old, no more.
In my stamp album, though, an Empire already glowed –
A worthy successor to Rome, with its countless tribes
Looking towards me, uniformed, smart, and proud.

Divided society, breeder of traitors and travesties,
Empty of purpose, empty of dignity –
Where has this fervour gone?

Midsummer Cornfield

Now almost lunchtime on a midsummer's azure day.
Nature has taunted and called through the lofty windows,
Too high to look out of, the whole morning long.
An aberrant bee has buzzed
Round each sill's captive flowers
Then flown teasingly to freedom.
Our rustic academy,
Focussed on blackboard and inkwell and page and pedagogue,
Has ground inexorably through its rituals.
There has been incantation of tables,
Practice of proud-nibbed copperplate,
Brow-furrowing arithmetic
And challenging, revealing compositions
('What I intend to do when I leave school').
But now we are almost through it all
And we have reached that final tidying-up
Arms-folded-when-you-are-ready electric moment
Before they let us go.

Suddenly we are off, as if released
By a pistol-shot into motion.
I am first to the door, my lunchtime package clutched
In one keen hand; lift up the heavy latch with the other,
Out through the cool stone porch, and I am free.
An assault of light: after the sad brown tiles,
Now jubilant greens and blues, and the shouts of flowers,
And pulsing parching heat, and the flood of birdsong.

I take the helm of my destiny: out of the playground,
Past the trim flanking cottages, then down Church Bank
Like the smooth bed of our torrent between lush shores
Of fragrant foliage, canopied over here and there,
Now dappled with the silhouettes of leaves, now clear
But for my agile shadow dancing beside me,
Merging with those of my cascading friends.

We have shot the rapids of the shelving lane, and now
We pour into flat calm in the old inn yard
And haul on the huge palm-polished handle
Of the cumbrous clanking gauchely gushing pump
That quenches thirsts, and half drowns the unwary:
Laughter at soused heads. Splutterings. Rusty tones
Of that crude iron weapon that is so welcoming.

Sated at last, and fit to brave the sun, we scatter:
Some of us take the pitted potholed track
Pointing out of the village, leading to fields
And timelessness, to blazing earth and sky.
At the waving cornfield's corner, in we plunge
Throw ourselves down to munch with youthful zest
And then to bathe in perfumes and pungencies,
Shrill thrilling frenzies of the soil's arousal,
Rankness of dank roots, scent of basking grain,
Chaotic chorus of crazed insect hordes
Besotted with the heat.

I hear and breathe all, face turned to the sky,
Head resting on cupped hands, eyes tightly closed
Gazing enrapt as rays rose-tint their lids
And, on that zephyred lake of rippling bronze
I loose my oars and let my limp limbs trail.
No shore is visible, no creaking chains
Grapple me to convention's unbudged anchor,
No compass nags me to my course.
Elation, like a smoothly lifting swell,
Buoys up my weightless raft of sumptuous dreams.
I glimpse, then melt into, my aery soul
And a lark's reckless ribbon of winged song
Pennons me through the heavens.

The Collective Launching

Thursdays were special. Then, old Squire Ralph's 'picture',
As he called his village, would gain an extra detail:
A feature blending in perfectly, gracing the scene
Of sweeping yew-tree and silent sedate Keele Farm
Mysterious beyond its beeches, its broad iron gate,
Its unvisited drive, and with that obstinate gable
Showing, like a stopped clock, 'eighteen sixty-two'.

There stood, on Thursdays, our elegant Riley saloon –
'Newcastle's miniature Rolls', some were wont to call it –
A creation of craftsmen's pride, its timbers worked
And panels curved by hand, a human presence
With harmonious lines exultant and full of life,
Dressed in discreet shades, black and deep maroon,
Though its wheels wore silver discs like a dandy's spats.

How proud I was to find it awaiting me
At the school day's end, how awed my fellows were
By this horseless carriage set down in their quiet domain.
The lads of the village watched as I climbed abroad,
Then they mustered at the stern and all hands heaved
To help in producing the miracle of motion
As our trim hull sailed off into open country.

So guileless was their goodwill that Father gladly
Accepted the proffered power – he who tuned his engine,
Like some maestro a Stradivarius, to do his bidding;
And who used to explore every inch of our Riley's paintwork,
Like a gallery director inspecting his priceless hoard!
Thus was my Thursday voyage out to Woore and Nantwich
Blessed by true hearts in the place I reverence still.

The Riley

Above: Enjoying rural peace near Baldwin's Gate;
Below: Parked by the war memorial at Hanmer, Flints.

(Photographs by the late Roland Higson)

The Vicar Taking Scripture

He vapoured in to us always once a week
Lofty and vague, with his head as if lost in mist,
And the most unmemorable voice, unmemorable theme.

He entered, yet did not enter, our inkstained world
Of prow-to-stern desks like captive roller-coasters
Gripped by the lofty-windowed brown-tiled walls;
Our pungencies scantly sponged, heads cropped to the forelock,
And virile clogs that struck sparks in the lane
Were no part of his more ethereal being.

He looked always rather frail as he glided in
As if on rails well polished, the points all set
By our martinet ma'ams who knew their business well.
Everything there was garnished for his coming:
The coke-stove stoked to choking, the black sheep scolded,
The blackmail manacles tautened like tourniquets
With the Friday afternoon treat, like a fickle mirage,
Threatening once more to dissolve at the first offence.

After such preparations as they made
He could have sleepwalked with impunity
Through his portentous, slightly unreal hour;
He could have hummed like wires, or screamed
Like a circular saw, or rattled his long blundering
Bones like castanets, or hissed steam
Through his ears, or his always half-unbuttoned flies.

We should have hung respectfully on his every absurdity
Who, if we had ever got him on his own,
Without those virulent, savagely biting sanctions
That held us down in almost feudal subjection,
Would have called, once for all, the bluff of his sanctity
And sent him home naked, martyred, mocked and mad !

The Old Keele Village School
Photographed during one of the author's many subsequent visits to Keele.

Intimations of Immorality

It was 'on this wise'
As the dignified old Bible would have said:
On this wise was my discovery of *loins*.

I was not much taller than a folio
And had been entirely immersed in childish things,
A happily submissive subject of my village school
Ruled by Miss Tennant, a wizened martinet
Straight as a beanpole and nudging her century.

Her grip was of iron, her visage inscrutable;
Benevolence there, but buried now deep, deep down.
Inflexible integrity had become her anchor.
Emotion there may have been once, and fleetingly,
But she'd been forced, long since, to choke it back.
She was like an Old Testament lawgiver
Who had somehow excluded love from the equation,
One of those heroically selfless pedagogues
Who give every hour and ounce of strength to their role
And end up tragically emptied automatons.

Though upright in all senses to the last
She had become, one felt it, frail as a husk
About to fall prey to the faintest winnowing breath.
Familiarity with her rituals
Only just held her in place.

Inevitably the winnower came,
A none too gentle one.
Son of a local farmer holding a grudge
Who primed the youth to stand up to her.
Unhaltingly he extruded his father's diatribe
While she paled and shook and raised her hand to strike

Then, with superb self-restraint,
As she identified the source,
Restored it to her side.

Presently he crouched, a wreck, after his outrage,
But it was she who left
Like a pale husk fluttering from his van,
To make way for new life.

Miss Downend was *it*!
As supple as the other was stiff,
As abundant as the other was shrunken,
As ripely carnal as the other was pinched and dry.

Her eyes, like a gun-dog's, gave off chilling fire
And deadly was her pursuit of the miscreant,
But her haughty carriage fought in vain to control
The wild roll of her hips, and when they rolled
Her haunches shook their extrovert amplitude –
What jellies, I thought, from what unsuspected moulds!

She was an orchard in August,
She was massed clusters of grapes –
And I was the patient!

Without noticing me she enslaved me,
My gaze was chained to her whenever she moved
Though I could not begin to diagnose why –
Knowing only that she had skill to become for moments
The beckoning molten centre of my world!

The tiny putto did not recognize Venus
Or the first breath of the madness of Baudelaire!

The Truant

Considering how few they were, and always women,
I marvel how our schooldames kept control;
Only one pupil was wholly beyond their curbing,
Because he had wounds and yearnings too deep to share.
Wild with frustration, they lashed his helpless silence
With sharp jibes while his pain grew tenser still
And became a scream though he could not breathe a sound.

Only once did I see contentment fill his face:
When, as our bus groaned slowly up Keele Bank
And the broad grim Potteries smokescape spread itself
Peered through by clean horizons far beyond,
He brightened and started to point excitedly
To sunlit landmarks he knew from those Odysseys
He had taken for weeks on end in lieu of school.

Quite carried away, he harangued us exultantly
About distance and freedom with sparkling dream-filled eyes
And we wondered at this brave, lone, tortured being
Who wanted only to run, while we conformed.
Then we noticed that someone else was listening too:
Upright Miss Jenkins, though several seats away
From his tall, thin, reeling, semaphoring figure,
Had caught the drift of his voyager's ecstasy
And turned to an exclamation-mark of ice!

A few days more and he was off again,
The obstinate eluder, this next evasion
His longest yet. They could not rein him in.
And when at last they held him, their rage boiled over
Into savage and self-defeating ridicule:
They had him roped, led everywhere by his fellows,
And mocked by all, like a suspect sulphurous Christ.
A little of that, and of course he fled once more,
Desperate for solitude, calm, and dignity.

Where is he now? I pray his pain has ceased,
That he has faced and struck back at his torment,
Has smashed his silence. Found his poet's voice.

Vanished Ghosts

Now I'm a man, and the last of the squires long perished;
Though even he was an unseen absentee
With scant faith in his order, a restless soul
Scudding about Society, making waves
In the tut-tut gossip sheets. His worthier sires
Had stayed at home, cultivating their garden,
As had his uncle Ralph, a squire indeed,
Fons et origo of the Keele I knew:
Creator of my school, my church, my inn,
My cottages, lodges, farms – a world renewed
At his deft fingers' touch to regale my childhood.

But I'm a man now, that last Sneyd long gone,
And squire's park turned into groves of Academe;
Cap-doffing rustics replaced by voracious minds
Lured from all over the globe to be poured into moulds
Of specialized skill in that Babel of building-styles
Alive with the buzz of jockeying disciplines.
Squire's Hall is still majestic but somehow empty
Like coral shaped by creatures whom time dissolved;
And my old school too is a shell, the action moved
To a clean new presentable building along the lane,
Fit for professors' precisely-spoken offspring.

Only at dusk do the chastened untouchables waken
And whisper in the older homelier structure.
Miss Tennant and Miss Jenkins and Miss Downend
Take up their wonted roles and echo onward
Stern in their stiffened ways, those passionate despots
Who aimed us towards the heights with love and fury.
But they are dust: in the first rays of sunrise
They falter and drift away, my school falls vacant,
The classrooms are vaults, the voiceless playgrounds voids.

Now I'm a man, have risen as if with wings
Eager to storm the heavens; but I now come home
To those whose wrists released me, those wondrous dames
Who, set in peasant soil, still quested starward.
None gave them proper praise, those valiant mentors
Who launched me with all the force that they could muster
Into the skies where merit might find favour.
I've ridden high, but pride is not my hallmark,

No belief in miraculous novelty turns my head;
Even Renaissance Man knew his all prefashioned
And reverenced the past as the bedrock of his being.

I honour them and their primitive seat of learning;
Yes, village and field and bird and beast and flower,
Nature and squire who had composed our backcloth,
But most those heroic tragedians who trod the boards
Before their groundlings' pernicious ingratitude.
Then, I was just a seed obsessed with growing,
With splitting the tight walls and bursting through;
Now, from beyond the wounded womb I ponder
My aching debt, too late to speak my thanks.

Remains of the old 'Three Mile'

> There is nothing at the end of the road
> better than may be found beside it.
> – EDWARD THOMAS

Vestige of a meander in my country lane,
'cut' by the straight-ruled travesty
that has succeeded you
defying poetry for speed,
I glimpse you still from the roadside –
a solitary pariah among lanes,
ostracized now by Man.

Yours was too voluptuous,
too wanton, too wayward a curve;
and the brutal puritans of economy
just had to gash it off
so that we can get to 'b'
that little bit sooner, and safer,
but joylessly.

I, who still walk, among the blinkered speeders,
walk slow as ever I did,
I call to you with my soul;
I dote on your still shimmering arc
whenever I pass by
among the robot semblances
too vain to feel or see.

Country Retrospect*

By Horsetrough Bank and Agger Hill
And Honeywall and Highway Lane,
Of heady heaven I had my fill
In kindly days before all pain.

Before my Fall, before I grew
To pine and groan with urban man,
Before my youth's elation knew
How fate can crush what well began,

Before they cast into the sky
Their deadly dust that fanned abroad
And tainted, fine and soft and sly,
The fields and woods a child adored.

On Horsetrough Bank and Agger Hill,
In Highway Lane and Honeywall,
I had an Eden at my will,
I had a bliss outclassing all.

And if you mock and if you doubt
My fond romantic's memory,
Then go and seek those places out
And ask the friends who ran with me,

And every one will say the same:
"He is no dreamer, he is right
To tell the story of our fame,
We did not suffer from your blight;

By Agger Hill and Horsetrough Bank,
By Honeywall and Highway Lane,
We shared the elixir that he drank
And would it could be shared again."

---

*The poem names real places in Madeley Heath and Keele as they were in 1941-3, shortly before a new (and possibly terminal) chapter of human history was opened by the horrors of Hiroshima and Nagasaki.

Keele Revisited

From church and lichgate still the lane leads down,
Plain-cottaged, past my school – serenely small
With stone-capped gable and with diapered wall
And squire's proud cipher as its graven crown;

Kind early cradle of my fool's renown
Where genial peasants were my comrades all,
Where I had space to heed the seasons' call
And swoon in fragrant corn and yearn to drown.

In those lost bounteous years that held no harm
This lane was vast, like heaven's protecting palm;
But now, so dwindled and so impotent,

It cannot help against my human foes –
Their rage half-crazed, their springs of solace spent,
Their purpose . . . neither God nor Nature knows.

Shadows

In trees and meadows, loins and babies' limbs,
The politicians stockpile strontium;
Nor can it aid us, now, to plumb the womb
And comb those verdant aisles where memory dims:

Above the pristine ease, the silent hymns
Of those green groves, that bland Elysium
Where new life beamed at aeons yet to come,
The screeching vulture of the present skims.

O, tireless summer of our infancy,
When with our agile forms exultantly
We painted sun-bright lane and fragrant field,

Your beatific vision, while we gaze,
By fate's grim palimpsest is soon concealed,
And shadows sprawl in fierce extinction's blaze.

Aubade

Striding down the spurside
past the birdbelfry trees,
the valley fledged with mist
soft on its sombre sleep,
the foreglow of a new day
edging across the heavens
like a calm conquering tide,

with my heart jolted true,
deepened like the sky's smooth dome
by the impact of love's wave,
I thrill to the ringing woods
while a firmament of birds
opens and comes aflame
with coruscating song.

No maze of mansound
muffles those crystal notes,
their echoing resonance
through the trees' naves,
through a world pristine made
for this brief nightspace,
in this first chorused dawn,

nature rejoicing now
at this clear hour of four,
wakening into a dream
of Eden-purity,
a green untainted realm
emptied of plaguethrong Man,
sure in its glories still.

December Landscape
(Whitmore)

Bare are the trees now by the stream's cool flow,
And yet their lichened trunks are verdant still;
The hardy hedge that skirts the church's hill
Still jests at death, its autumn bronze aglow.

The curving weir, in summer bored and slow,
Fed by the copious lake with spates that thrill,
Shakes out its glistening tresses with a will
And in contented tones it murmurs low.

Now, clear and sharp and vibrant is the air
Like youth's first reckless mad-kissed love-affair;
Now, branches twine their proud anatomies

Defiant of the threatening rime and snow
As wanton satyrs, coupling as they please,
Might mock some old and soured Malvolio!

Students exploring Keele Village